How to Use This Book

A Variety of Presentations

1. Make overhead transparencies of the lessons. Present each lesson as an oral activity with the entire class. Write answers and make corrections using an erasable marker.

   As the class becomes more familiar with *Daily Word Problems*, have students mark their answers first and then check them against correct responses marked on the transparency.

2. Reproduce the problems for individuals or partners to work on independently. Check answers as a group, using an overhead transparency to model the solutions' strategies. (Use these pages as independent practice only after much group experience with the lessons.)

3. Occasionally you may want to reproduce problems as a test to see how individuals are progressing in their acquisition of skills.

Important Considerations

1. Allow students to use whatever tools they need to solve problems. Some students will choose to use manipulatives, while others will want to make drawings.

2. It is important that students share their solutions. Modeling a variety of problem-solving techniques makes students aware that there are different paths to the correct answer. Don't scrimp on the amount of time allowed for discussing how solutions were reached.

3. Teach students to follow problem-solving strategies:
   • Read the problem carefully more than one time. Think about it as you read.
   • Mark the important information in the problem.
      What question does the problem ask?

      What words will help you know how to solve the problem (*in all, left, how many more*, etc.)?

      What facts will help you answer the question? (Cross out facts that are NOT needed.)
   • Think about what you need to do to solve the problem (add, subtract, multiply).
   • Solve the problem. Does your answer make sense?
   • Check your answer.

Scope and Sequence–Grade 2

Week	1	2	3	4	5	6	7	8	9	10	11	12	13	14	15	16	17	18	19	20	21	22	23	24	25	26	27	28	29	30	31	32	33	34	35	36
Addition Facts	•	•	•		•	•	•	•							•	•			•	•	•	•		•				•			•					
Subtraction Facts	•	•	•		•	•	•			•	•	•	•	•	•				•			•					•		•	•	•		•	•	•	•
Column Addition	•	•								•	•	•	•	•				•			•	•		•	•			•		•	•	•	•	•	•	•
2-Digit Addition with No Regrouping							•			•				•			•	•				•			•						•					
2-Digit Subtraction with No Regrouping			•	•					•	•	•		•			•		•				•														•
2-Digit Addition with Regrouping						•	•	•	•				•					•		•		•	•	•	•	•	•	•	•	•	•	•	•	•		•
2-Digit Subtraction with Regrouping														•	•		•		•	•	•		•	•	•	•		•	•	•	•	•	•	•	•	•
3-Digit Addition and Subtraction						•							•	•		•				•	•	•	•	•	•	•	•	•	•	•	•	•	•	•	•	•
Multiplication																•				•	•	•	•	•				•	•						•	
Count by Twos					•					•		•								•	•	•														
Count by Fives				•	•				•		•		•	•			•	•	•							•								•		
Count by Tens				•				•					•																	•						
Fractions	•				•	•	•	•	•			•	•		•	•					•	•		•	•					•				•		
Time	•	•				•														•				•	•			•		•						•
Money	•	•						•	•	•	•					•				•			•		•		•	•			•	•		•		•
Use Tally Marks																•																				
Read and Interpret Graphs and Charts	•	•			•				•			•				•				•					•				•	•		•	•	•		
Read Number Words	•	•	•						•		•										•	•	•	•	•	•		•		•			•		•	•

Daily Word Problems

Monday-Week 5

A Picnic

Goldilocks had a picnic. She asked the Three Bears to come. She asked the Seven Dwarfs, too.

How many guests did she ask?

Name: _____

Work Space:

Answer:

_____ guests

Daily Word Problems

Tuesday-Week 5

A Picnic

Mother made 18 peanut butter sandwiches and 12 egg sandwiches for the picnic. 9 peanut butter sandwiches were eaten.

How many peanut butter sandwiches were left?

Name: _____

Work Space:

Answer:

_____ peanut butter sandwiches

Daily Word Problems
Wednesday-Week 5

A Picnic

The picnic lasted 3 hours.

If it started at 2 o'clock, at what time did it end?

Name:

Work Space:

Show your answer on the clock.

Answer:

_____ o'clock

Daily Word Problems
Thursday-Week 5

A Picnic

Each of the Seven Dwarfs ate 2 cookies. Each of the Three Bears ate 2 brownies.

How many more cookies were eaten than brownies?

Name:

Work Space:

Answer:

_____ cookies

Name:

Goldilocks made a chart to show how much food was eaten at her picnic.

peanut butter sandwiches	///// /////
egg sandwiches	///// //
cookies	///// ///// /////
brownies	///// /
carrot sticks	///// /////
orange juice	///// //
apple juice	///// ///// //

Remember: ///// = 5

1. How many more cookies than brownies were eaten?

      _____ cookies

2. How many sandwiches were eaten in all?

      _____ sandwiches

Daily Word Problems

Monday-Week 6

Nature Walk

Jakob went for a walk in the woods with Grandpa. They left home at 1 o'clock. "Be back in 2 hours," said Jakob's mother.

At what time did they have to be back?

Name: _____

Work Space:

Show your answer on the clock.

Answer:

_____ o'clock

Daily Word Problems

Tuesday-Week 6

Nature Walk

Jakob and Grandpa saw 6 birds and 3 squirrels. They saw 5 rabbits and 1 snake.

How many animals did they see on the walk?

Name: _____

Work Space:

Answer:

_____ animals

Daily Word Problems

Wednesday-Week 6

Nature Walk

Grandpa and Jakob saw a squirrel picking up nuts.
12 nuts were on the ground. The squirrel took 7 of the nuts away.

How many nuts were still on the ground?

Name:

Work Space:

Answer:

_____ nuts

Daily Word Problems

Thursday-Week 6

Nature Walk

Jakob likes to go on walks with Grandpa. Last month they walked on nine days. This month they walked on eight days.

On how many days did they walk in the two months?

Name:

Work Space:

Answer:

_____ days

Name:

Nature Walk

Grandpa took lunch out of his backpack.
He had two sandwiches and four cookies.
He gave half of the lunch to Jakob.

How many did Grandpa give Jakob?

_____ sandwich

_____ cookies

Color the things Jakob ate.

Daily Word Problems

Monday-Week 7

Pet Fish

Walter has three blue fish and two red fish. Kim has one black fish. Norma has eight goldfish.

How many more fish does Norma have than Walter?

Name:

Work Space:

Answer:

_____ fish

Daily Word Problems

Tuesday-Week 7

Pet Fish

Walter got more pet fish. He needed a bigger tank for his fish. The new tank cost $8.00. Walter paid with two $5.00 bills.

How much change did he get back?

Name:

Work Space:

Answer:

$_____

Daily Word Problems

Pet Fish

Walter uses ½ of a box of fish food in a week. Norma uses ¼ of a box of fish food in a week.

Who uses the most fish food?

Name:

Work Space:

Answer:

_____ uses the most fish food.

Daily Word Problems

Pet Fish

One of Walter's fish had 14 babies. He gave half of the babies to Norma.

How many fish did Walter give her?

Name:

Work Space:

Answer:

_____ fish

Walter measured his pet fish. He made this chart to show how long the fish were.

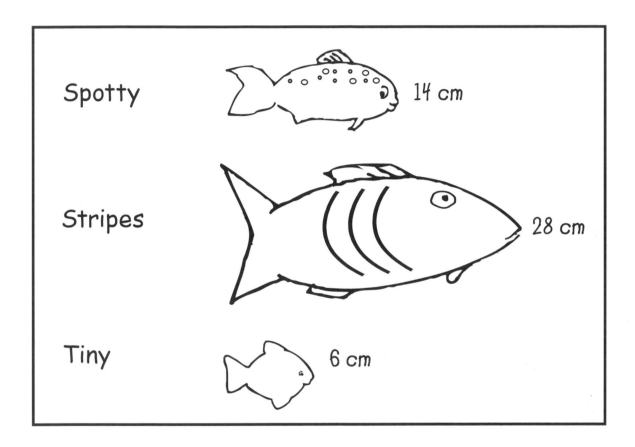

Spotty — 14 cm

Stripes — 28 cm

Tiny — 6 cm

1. How much longer is Stripes than Spotty? _____ cm

2. How much longer is Spotty than Tiny? _____ cm

Daily Word Problems

Soup

Maggie wanted chicken noodle soup for lunch. One can of soup made 4 servings. Maggie ate two servings. Her mother ate one serving.

How much soup was left?

Name:

Work Space:

Answer:

_____ serving

Daily Word Problems

Soup

Soup is on sale at the market. I can buy 2 cans for $1.00.

How much will I pay if I buy 4 cans?

Name:

Work Space:

Answer:

$_____

Daily Word Problems
Wednesday–Week 8

Soup

Father likes to make homemade soup. This is what he bought for his soup.

    6 carrots
    1 onion
    4 potatoes
    7 green beans

How many vegetables did he use in all?

Name:

Work Space:

Answer:

_____ vegetables

Daily Word Problems
Thursday–Week 8

Soup

Father bought rolls to go with the soup he made. Each roll cost 10¢.

How much did Father pay for six rolls?

Name:

Work Space:

Answer:

_____ ¢

Soup

Maggie asked 8 friends, "Do you want chicken soup, tomato soup, or pea soup?" $\frac{1}{2}$ wanted chicken soup. $\frac{1}{4}$ wanted tomato soup. The rest wanted pea soup.

Color the bowls green to show how many friends wanted **pea soup**.

Daily Word Problems

Monday-Week 9

The Bakery

Tina went to the bakery for her mother. She bought one dozen small cookies and five large cookies.

How many more small cookies than large cookies did Tina buy?

Name:

Work Space:

Answer:

_____ small cookies

Daily Word Problems

Tuesday-Week 9

The Bakery

The baker sold 5 cupcakes, 6 muffins, and 9 rolls to Mrs. Lee.

How many treats did Mrs. Lee buy?

Name:

Work Space:

Answer:

_____ treats

Daily Word Problems

Wednesday-Week 9

The Bakery

If one cookie costs 5¢, how many can you buy with a quarter?

Name:

Work Space:

Answer:

_____ cookies

Daily Word Problems

Thursday-Week 9

The Bakery

Pete had eight cookies. He gave $\frac{1}{4}$ of the cookies to Bob.

How many cookies did he have left?

Name:

Work Space:

Color $\frac{1}{4}$ of these cookies brown.

Answer:

_____ cookies

Daily Word Problems • EMC 3002

Name:

Cookie   5¢

Muffin   10¢

Tart   30¢

1. What can I buy if I have a dime and six pennies?

_____

2. How many cookies can I buy with 6 nickels?

_____ cookies

3. I bought two muffins. I paid with a quarter. How much change will I get back?

_____ ¢

Daily Word Problems

Monday-Week 10

Snacks

Marcus likes pickles a lot. Yesterday he ate 3 dill pickles, 4 sweet pickles, and 3 bread-and-butter pickles. Today he ate twice as many pickles.

How many pickles did Marcus eat today?

Name:

Work Space:

Answer:

_____ pickles

Daily Word Problems

Tuesday-Week 10

Snacks

Jan and her friends wanted popcorn after school. Mom made 15 cups of popcorn. The girls ate 12 cups.

How many cups of popcorn were left?

Name:

Work Space:

Answer:

_____ cups of popcorn

Daily Word Problems
Wednesday-Week 10

Snacks

Pete had 12 peanuts. He gave $\frac{1}{3}$ of the peanuts to Bill.

How many peanuts did he give Bill?

Name:

Work Space:

Color the peanuts Pete gave Bill.

Answer:

_____ peanuts

Daily Word Problems
Thursday-Week 10

Snacks

My Brownie troop ate sandwiches after our meeting. Each sandwich had 2 slices of bread.

How many slices of bread did it take to make 9 sandwiches?

Name:

Work Space:

Answer:

_____ slices of bread

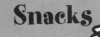

Snacks

Today's Special Snacks

pickles	60¢
popcorn	30¢
peanuts	70¢
pretzels	50¢

Arnold wanted a snack. He went to the store to buy something. He looked at what things cost. He had 85¢. He bought two snacks.

What did he buy?

_____

Daily Word Problems

Clowns

Name:

Work Space:

A funny car stopped in the circus ring. Out came a dozen clowns. Four of the clowns were tall. The rest were short.

How many short clowns were there?

Answer:

_____ short clowns

Daily Word Problems

Clowns

Name:

Work Space:

Bobo the clown has many trained animals. He has 20 dogs, 12 cats, and 26 mice.

How many animals does Bobo have in all?

Answer:

_____ animals

Daily Word Problems

Wednesday–Week 11

Clowns

Arturo and Miguel went to the circus to see the clowns. The show started at 2:30. It lasted 3 hours.

At what time was the show over?

Name: _____

Work Space:

Show your answer on the clock.

Answer:

_____ **:** _____

Daily Word Problems

Thursday–Week 11

Clowns

The ringmaster measured the clowns in his circus. The tallest clown was 76 inches tall. The shortest clown was 54 inches tall.

How much taller was the tallest clown than the shortest clown?

Name: _____

Work Space:

Answer:

_____ inches

Name:

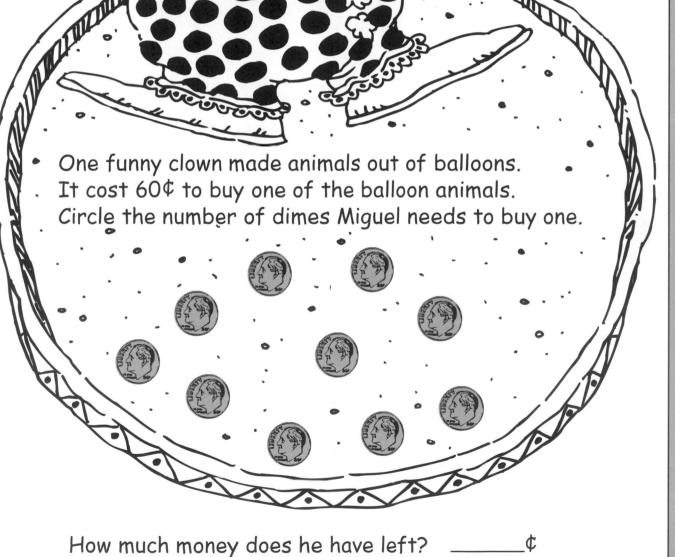

One funny clown made animals out of balloons.
It cost 60¢ to buy one of the balloon animals.
Circle the number of dimes Miguel needs to buy one.

How much money does he have left? _____¢

Daily Word Problems

Monday-Week 12

Kites

Mr. Wong had 24 blue kites, 22 red kites, and 13 orange kites for sale.

How many kites did he have for sale?

Name:

Work Space:

Answer:

_____ kites

Daily Word Problems

Tuesday-Week 12

Kites

15 children took kites to the park. 9 of the children were boys.

How many girls took kites to the park?

Name:

Work Space:

Answer:

_____ girls

Daily Word Problems

Wednesday-Week 12

Kites

Sally bought a kite. She paid this much money.

How much did her kite cost?

Name:

Work Space:

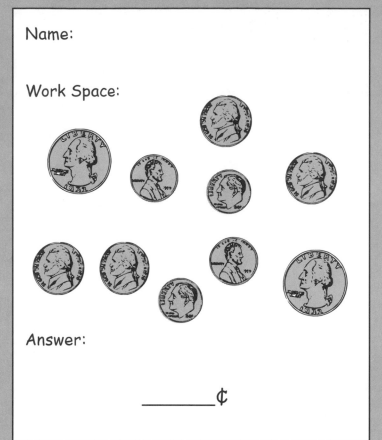

Answer:

_____ ¢

Daily Word Problems

Thursday-Week 12

Kites

Clara took her kite to the park at 3:00. She had to be home in an hour and a half.

At what time did she have to be home?

Name:

Work Space:

Show your answer on the clock.

Answer:

_____:_____

Daily Word Problems

Friday-Week 12

Name: _____

Kites

This graph tells about the colors of kites children were flying in the park. Each kite picture stands for 2 kites. Use the graph to help you answer the questions.

Colorful Kites

red	
blue	
purple	
green	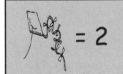 = 2

1. How many more children have red kites than purple kites? _____ children

2. How many children have kites? _____ children

Daily Word Problems

Monday–Week 13

Pets at School

Our teacher let us bring our pets to school. Colby brought his pet snake. When he got the snake it was 12 inches long. Now it is 32 inches long.

How much has the snake grown?

Name:

Work Space:

Answer:

_____ inches

Tuesday–Week 13

Pets at School

Maria brought her cats Fluffy and Samson to school. Maria is 7 years old. Fluffy is 6 years old. Samson is 9 years older than Fluffy.

How old is Samson?

Name:

Work Space:

Answer:

_____ years old

Daily Word Problems

Wednesday-Week 13

Pets at School

Name:

Work Space:

Rani brought her pet parrot Squawk to class. Squawk has been in Rani's family for 26 years.

If Squawk was 13 years old when the family got him, how old is Squawk now?

Answer:

_____ years old

Daily Word Problems

Thursday-Week 13

Pets at School

Name:

Work Space:

Sidney showed his pet hens Ginger and Cluck to the class. Each hen lays an egg almost every day. Last year Ginger laid 234 eggs and Cluck laid 245 eggs.

How many eggs did the hens lay last year?

Answer:

_____ eggs

Daily Word Problems
Friday-Week 13

Pets at School

Mr. Blake asked the class, "What pets do you have?"
This is what he found out.

 7 children had dogs.

 5 children had cats.

 1 child had a fish.

 2 children had hamsters.

 2 children had birds.

 1 child had a snake.

 8 children had no pets.

Then Mr. Blake asked, "How many more
children have pets than do **not** have pets?" _____ children

Daily Word Problems

Monday–Week 14

Play Ball

23 girls and 36 boys played ball at recess.

How many students played ball?

Daily Word Problems

Tuesday–Week 14

Play Ball

We got new balls for every classroom. Each class got 1 basketball, 1 baseball, 2 kickballs, and 1 soccer ball.

1. How many balls did each class get?

2. How many balls were needed for 10 classes?

Daily Word Problems
Wednesday-Week 14

Play Ball

Some boys had a contest during recess. Bob made twelve baskets. Raul made ten baskets. Leroy made fourteen baskets.

How many baskets did the boys make in all?

Name:

Work Space:

Answer:

_____ baskets

Daily Word Problems
Thursday-Week 14

Play Ball

Kanisha's parents gave her a soccer ball. The soccer ball cost $23.00. Father gave the clerk $25.00.

How much change did he get back?

Name:

Work Space:

Answer:

$_____

Name:

Play Ball

The kids in my neighborhood love to play ball games.

Ball Games

Six kids play basketball and soccer.

Nine kids play baseball and soccer.

Two kids play soccer, baseball, and bowling.

1. What game do the most kids play? _____

2. How many more kids play soccer than basketball? _____ kids

Daily Word Problems
Monday-Week 15

Summer Fun

154 boys and 202 girls are going to day camp.

How many children is that?

Name:

Work Space:

Answer:

_____ children

Daily Word Problems
Tuesday-Week 15

Summer Fun

It costs $45.00 for a week at camp. Sid has only $30.00.

How much more money does he need?

Name:

Work Space:

Answer:

$_____

Daily Word Problems • EMC 3002

Daily Word Problems

Wednesday-Week 15

Summer Fun

Sid and his best friends are having a dog wash to earn money for camp. They started washing dogs at 1:30. They stopped at 4:30.

How many hours did they wash dogs?

Name:

Work Space:

Answer:

_____ hours

Daily Word Problems

Thursday-Week 15

Summer Fun

Sid and Mollie each washed 7 dogs. Henry and Pablo each washed 6 dogs.

How many dogs did the children wash in all?

Name:

Work Space:

Answer:

_____ dogs

Dog Wash

big	$3.00
medium	$2.00
small	$1.00

1. Mollie and Sid washed 2 big dogs, 2 medium-sized dogs, and 3 small dogs. How much money did they make? $_____

2. Pablo and Henry washed 1 big dog, 2 medium-sized dogs, and 3 small dogs. How much money did they make? $_____

3. How much money did the children make in all? $_____

Daily Word Problems

Monday-Week 16

At the Movies

Alex, Tony, and Maggie want to see a dinosaur movie. A ticket will cost $2.00 for each of them.

How much will it cost the children to see the movie?

Name:

Work Space:

Answer:

$ _____

Daily Word Problems

Tuesday-Week 16

At the Movies

Maggie had 78¢. She bought a small soda that cost 55¢.

How much money did she have left?

Name:

Work Space:

Answer:

_____ ¢

Daily Word Problems

Wednesday-Week 16

At the Movies

The dinosaur movie started 2 hours ago. It is now 4:00.

At what time did the movie start?

Name:

Work Space:

Show your answer on the clock.

Answer:

_____:_____

Daily Word Problems

Thursday-Week 16

At the Movies

Tony and Maggie walked 9 blocks home. Alex walked twice as far.

How many blocks did he walk home?

Name:

Work Space:

Answer:

_____ blocks

Mr. Cruz asked his students, "What kinds of movies do you like?"

This is what they answered.

dinosaur movies	/// /// /
western movies	/// //
comedies	///
scary movies	//
outer space movies	///

1. What kind of movie did the most children like? _____

2. What kind of movie was least popular? _____

3. How many more children liked dinosaur movies than scary movies? _____

4. How many children are shown on the chart? _____

Make a tally mark by your favorite kind of movie.

Daily Word Problems

Monday-Week 17

Strongest Kid

Marcus is the strongest kid in second grade. He used to lift 12 pounds. Now he can lift 97 pounds.

How much more can he lift now?

Name:

Work Space:

Answer:

_____ pounds

Daily Word Problems

Tuesday-Week 17

Strongest Kid

Marcus can do 1 chin-up every five seconds.

How long will it take him to do 9 chin-ups?

Name:

Work Space:

Answer:

_____ seconds

Daily Word Problems

Wednesday-Week 17

Strongest Kid

Marcus did 33 sit-ups this morning. Then he did 26 this afternoon.

How many sit-ups did he do today?

Name:

Work Space:

Answer:

_____ sit-ups

Daily Word Problems

Thursday-Week 17

Strongest Kid

Marcus rides his exercise bike 10 minutes each morning.

How many minutes does he ride in a week?

Name:

Work Space:

Answer:

_____ minutes

Name:

My friends and I like to exercise.
Some of us do sit-ups.
Some of us do chin-ups.
Some of us do both.

= 2 children

Sit-ups

Both

Chin-ups

How many more do sit-ups than chin-ups? _____ children

Daily Word Problems

Monday-Week 18

Raccoons

Raccoons fish for crayfish in the creek by Otto's farm. Otto likes to hide and watch the raccoons. One night the raccoons caught 36 crayfish. The next night they caught 23 crayfish.

How many more did they catch on the first night?

Name:

Work Space:

Answer:

_____ crayfish

Daily Word Problems

Tuesday-Week 18

Raccoons

There were 10 mother raccoons in the woods. Each mother raccoon had 7 babies.

How many raccoon babies is that in all?

Name:

Work Space:

Answer:

_____ babies

Daily Word Problems

Wednesday-Week 18

Raccoons

If it is very cold, raccoons stay in a den during most of the winter. There were 25 raccoons in one den. There were 15 raccoons in another den.

How many raccoons stayed in dens?

Name:

Work Space:

Answer:

_____ raccoons

Daily Word Problems

Thursday-Week 18

Raccoons

A raccoon stays in its den most of the day. At night it comes out to look for food. One raccoon came out of its den at 8:15. It looked for food for 3 hours.

At what time did it go back into its den?

Name:

Work Space:

Show your answer on the clock.

Answer:

____ : ____

Daily Word Problems

Friday-Week 18

Raccoons

Ranger Pete counted the raccoons that came to the river in the park. In five weeks he saw this many raccoons.

Raccoon Sightings

Week	Raccoons
Week 1	10
Week 2	10
Week 3	15
Week 4	10
Week 5	5

1. How many raccoons did Ranger Pete see in all?

   _____ raccoons

2. How many more did he see in Week 3 than in Week 5?

   _____ raccoons

Daily Word Problems

Monday–Week 19

Nuts!

Mrs. Smith's Nut Shop sells all kinds of nuts. She sells walnuts in little bags. Each bag holds 5 walnuts.

How many walnuts are in 8 bags?

Name:

Work Space:

Answer:

_____ walnuts

Daily Word Problems

Tuesday–Week 19

Nuts!

Peanuts cost 45¢ a bag.

How much will two bags cost?

Name:

Work Space:

Answer:

_____ ¢

Daily Word Problems

Wednesday-Week 19

Nuts!

A can of nuts costs $1.00. There are 15 walnuts, 11 pecans, and 43 peanuts in the can of nuts.

How many nuts are in one can?

Name:

Work Space:

Answer:

_____ nuts

Daily Word Problems

Thursday-Week 19

Nuts!

The Nut Shop opens at 8:00. Mrs. Smith closes the shop for lunch at 12:00.

How many hours is the shop open before lunch?

Name:

Work Space:

Answer:

_____ hours

Daily Word Problems

Friday–Week 19

Nuts!

This graph shows how many bags of nuts
Mrs. Smith sold today.

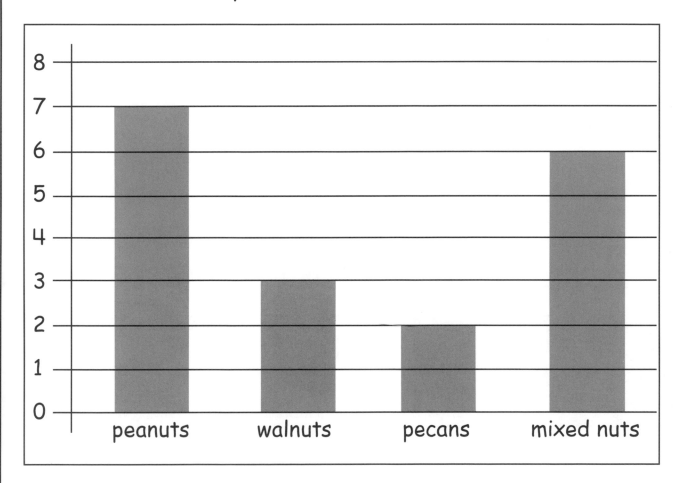

1. How many more bags of peanuts
   were sold than walnuts?   _____ bags of peanuts

2. How many fewer bags of pecans
   were sold than mixed nuts?   _____ bags of pecans

3. How many bags of nuts were
   sold in all?   _____ bags of nuts

Color a box on the graph to show the kind of nuts you would buy.

Daily Word Problems

Monday—Week 20

Balloons

The Balloon Man had 15 monkey balloons, 23 striped balloons, and 44 round balloons.

How many balloons did he have?

Name:

Work Space:

Answer:

_____ balloons

Daily Word Problems

Tuesday—Week 20

Balloons

One Saturday the Balloon Man sold 32 balloons. On Sunday he sold 40 balloons.

How many more balloons did he sell on Sunday?

Name:

Work Space:

Answer:

_____ balloons

Daily Word Problems

Wednesday-Week 20

Balloons

Max bought 9 balloons for his sister's birthday party. $\frac{1}{3}$ of the balloons got loose and flew away.

How many balloons flew away?

Name:

Work Space:

Color the balloons that got away.

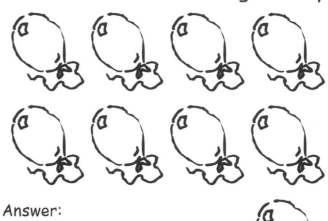

Answer:

_____ balloons

Daily Word Problems

Thursday-Week 20

Balloons

The Balloon Man went to work at 2:45. He stopped work an hour later.

At what time did he stop?

Name:

Work Space:

Show your answer on the clock.

Answer:

_____ : _____

Look at the Balloon Man's sign. Then answer the questions.

Balloons For Sale

Round Balloon
25¢

Monkey Balloon
$2.00

Striped Balloon
$1.00

1. Which balloon costs the most? _____

2. Which balloon costs the least? _____

3. How much would 4 monkey
   balloons cost? $_____

4. How much would one striped balloon
   and one round balloon cost? $_____

Daily Word Problems
Monday-Week 21

Bikes

There are 379 students in school. 261 have a bike.

How many **don't** have bikes?

Name:

Work Space:

Answer:

_____ students

Daily Word Problems
Tuesday-Week 21

Bikes

It is two miles from Tamara's house to school. She rides her bike to school and back home every day.

1. How many miles does she ride in one day?

2. How many miles does she ride in five days?

Name:

Work Space:

Answer:

1. _____ miles in one day

2. _____ miles in five days

Daily Word Problems

Wednesday-Week 21

Bikes

200 students never ride bikes to school. 73 students ride bikes to school every day. 126 ride bikes to school sometimes.

How many students ride bikes to school?

Name:

Work Space:

Answer:

_____ students

Daily Word Problems

Thursday-Week 21

Bikes

26 children in Tamara's neighborhood ride bikes. 18 of the children wear helmets.

How many children do **not** wear helmets?

Name:

Work Space:

Answer:

_____ children

Daily Word Problems

Friday-Week 21

Name:

Bikes

All six children in my family have bike helmets.

- ½ of the children have red helmets.
- ⅓ have blue helmets.

Color these helmets to show how many are red and how many are blue.

Daily Word Problems

Monday-Week 22

Apples

There was a big sign by the apple farm. The sign said "You pick, $2.00 a basket - We pick, $3.00 a basket."

If I picked three baskets of apples, what would I pay?

Name:

Work Space:

Answer:

$ _____

Daily Word Problems

Tuesday-Week 22

Apples

Max and Terry went to pick apples. Max picked one dozen apples. Terry picked two dozen apples.

How many apples did they pick in all?

Name:

Work Space:

Answer:

_____ apples

Daily Word Problems

Wednesday–Week 22

Apples

My Uncle George loves apples. On Friday he picked 43 apples. On Saturday he picked 31 apples. On Sunday he picked 25 apples.

How many apples did he pick in all?

Name: _____

Work Space:

Answer:

_____ apples

Daily Word Problems

Thursday–Week 22

Apples

Grandma had 18 apples. She used ½ of the apples to make a pie.

1. How many apples did she have left?

2. If Grandma made 2 pies, how many apples would she need?

Name: _____

Work Space:

Answer:

1. _____ apples left

2. _____ apples for 2 pies

Name:

Apples

Anna, Max, and Louis each made an apple pie.

Anna cut her apple pie in half.
Max cut his apple pie into fourths.
Louis cut his apple pie into thirds.

Mark these pies to show how they were cut.

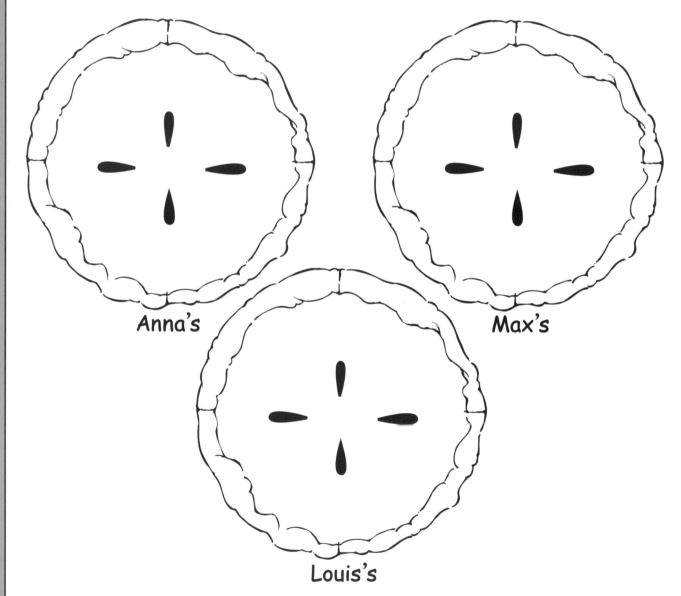

Anna's

Max's

Louis's

How many more pieces did Max have than Anna? _____ pieces

Daily Word Problems

Monday-Week 23

Collections

Ellen collects animal stickers. She has

30 cat stickers,
24 dog stickers,
22 mouse stickers, and
13 bird stickers.

How many stickers does she have in her collection?

Name:

Work Space:

Answer:

_____ stickers

Daily Word Problems

Tuesday-Week 23

Collections

Henry and Jerome collect stamps. Henry has 216 stamps. Jerome has 479 stamps.

How many fewer stamps does Henry have than Jerome?

Name:

Work Space:

Answer:

_____ stamps

Daily Word Problems

Wednesday-Week 23

Collections

Betty collects bears. She has 28 stuffed bears. She has 12 glass bears.

How many bears does she have in all?

Name:

Work Space:

Answer:

_____ bears

Daily Word Problems

Thursday-Week 23

Collections

Steve has 40 trading cards. Rachel has 10 more than Steve. Carlos has 10 more than Rachel.

How many trading cards does Carlos have?

Name:

Work Space:

Answer:

_____ trading cards

Peggy collects bird stickers. The stickers cost different amounts. This chart tells how much Peggy paid for each sticker.

Robin 15¢

Canary 20¢

Crow 50¢

Blue Jay 28¢

Quail 43¢

Toucan 65¢

1. How much more did the toucan sticker cost than the canary sticker? _____¢

2. How much would two blue jay stickers cost? _____¢

3. How much less did one robin sticker cost than a quail sticker? _____¢

Daily Word Problems
Monday–Week 24

Elephants

There were 5 baby elephants in the herd. There were twice as many adult elephants.

How many elephants were in the herd?

Name:

Work Space:

Answer:

_____ elephants

Daily Word Problems
Tuesday–Week 24

Elephants

An elephant can live to be 60 years old.

If an elephant is 42 years old, how long will it be until it is 60?

Name:

Work Space:

Answer:

_____ years

Daily Word Problems

Wednesday-Week 24

Elephants

The elephant calf weighed 265 pounds when it was born. Now it weighs 387 pounds.

How many pounds has it gained?

Name:

Work Space:

Answer:

_____ pounds

Daily Word Problems

Thursday-Week 24

Elephants

The elephants in the zoo ate 46 bales of hay yesterday. They ate 28 bales of hay today.

How much hay did they eat in two days?

Name:

Work Space:

Answer:

_____ bales of hay

Daily Word Problems

Friday-Week 24

Elephants

If one elephant has 2 ears, how many ears will 4 elephants have?

_____ ears

If one elephant has 4 legs, how many legs will 3 elephants have?

_____ legs

If one elephant has 2 tusks, how many tusks will 5 elephants have?

_____ tusks

If one elephant has 0 wings, how many wings will 2 elephants have?

_____ wings

Daily Word Problems

Monday-Week 25

Ice Cream

The ice-cream truck comes down our block at 2:30 every day. It is 2:05.

How many minutes do the children have to wait?

Name:

Work Space:

Answer:

_____ minutes

Daily Word Problems

Tuesday-Week 25

Ice Cream

There are 28 children on our block. Today 19 children bought ice cream.

How many children did **not** buy ice cream?

Name:

Work Space:

Answer:

_____ children

Daily Word Problems

Wednesday-Week 25

Ice Cream

Sixteen children bought ice-cream cones. Eleven children bought ice-cream bars. Three children bought ice-cream cups.

How many ice creams did the children buy in all?

Name:

Work Space:

Answer:

_____ ice creams

Daily Word Problems

Thursday-Week 25

Ice Cream

On Saturday the ice-cream man sold 124 ice creams. On Sunday he sold 163 ice creams.

How many did he sell in all?

Name:

Work Space:

Answer:

_____ ice creams

Tori and Sam looked at the chart to see what they could buy.

Ice Cream

Ice-Cream Cone
55¢

Popsicle
30¢

Ice-Cream Bar
40¢

Ice-Cream Cup
25¢

1. How much will it cost to buy a cone and a bar?   _____¢

2. How much will it cost to buy a bar, a cup, and a popsicle?   _____¢

3. How much more will it cost to buy a bar than a cup?   _____¢

4. "I want to buy ice cream for my two sisters and myself," said Tori. "I have 75¢. What can I buy?" Circle your answer.

3 cones

3 popsicles

3 bars

3 cups

Daily Word Problems

Monday-Week 26

Frogs

There are 24 frogs in the water and 13 frogs on lily pads. There are 42 more frogs on the bank of the river.

How many more frogs are on the bank than on lily pads?

Name:

Work Space:

Answer:

_____ frogs

Daily Word Problems

Tuesday-Week 26

Frogs

Frogs laid 497 eggs in the water. 165 eggs hatched.

How many eggs have **not** hatched?

Name:

Work Space:

Answer:

_____ eggs

Daily Word Problems

Wednesday-Week 26

Frogs

There were 7 frogs eating insects. Each frog ate 5 insects.

How many insects did the frogs eat in all?

Name:

Work Space:

Answer:

_____ insects

Daily Word Problems

Thursday-Week 26

Frogs

Freddy Frog was very hungry. This morning he ate 36 insects. This afternoon he ate 56 insects.

How many insects did Freddy eat today?

Name:

Work Space:

Answer:

_____ insects

Name:

Frogs

Write word problems about this picture. Show how to find the answers.

Write an addition word problem.

Write a subtraction word problem.

Write a multiplication word problem.

Daily Word Problems

Monday-Week 27

Happy Birthday

We are getting ready for Grandma's birthday party. Today we bought pretty paper for 56¢ and a bow for 35¢ so we can wrap her present.

How much did we spend in all?

Name:

Work Space:

Answer:

_____¢

Daily Word Problems

Tuesday-Week 27

Happy Birthday

We bought Grandma a card for her birthday. The card cost 63¢. We paid 70¢.

How much change did we get back?

Name:

Work Space:

Answer:

_____¢

Daily Word Problems

Wednesday-Week 27

Happy Birthday

Today is Grandma's birthday. She is 53 years old. Grandma is 7 years younger than Grandpa.

How old is Grandpa?

Name:

Work Space:

Answer:

_____ years old

Daily Word Problems

Thursday-Week 27

Happy Birthday

Grandma had a big birthday cake. There were 53 candles on the cake. Grandma cut the cake into 50 pieces.

How many pieces of cake were left after 37 pieces were eaten?

Name:

Work Space:

Answer:

_____ pieces of cake

Everybody in our family has a birthday in the same five months.

Grandpa–January 6

Uncle Jim–March 4

Carl–March 20

Grandma–April 15

Aunt Mary–May 19

Maggie–March 1

Dad–February 12

Uncle Frank–May 3

Sam–January 2

Mom–March 28

Jessie–February 11

Tony–May 16

*And my birthday is February 14, Valentine's Day.

Make tally marks to count how many birthdays are in each month.

January _____   February _____   March _____

April _____   May _____

1. Which month has the most birthdays?   _____

2. How many birthdays do we
   celebrate in that month?   _____ birthdays

Daily Word Problems

Monkey Fun

19 monkeys were sitting under a tree. 12 monkeys were swinging in the tree.

How many monkeys were there in all?

Name:

Work Space:

Answer:

_____ monkeys

Daily Word Problems

Monkey Fun

Four monkeys found a banana tree. Each monkey ate five bananas.

How many bananas did the monkeys eat in all?

Name:

Work Space:

Answer:

_____ bananas

Daily Word Problems
Wednesday-Week 28

Monkey Fun

There were 21 bananas in a bunch. One greedy monkey ate 15 bananas before his tummy began to hurt.

How many bananas were left?

Name:

Work Space:

Answer:

_____ bananas

Daily Word Problems
Thursday-Week 28

Monkey Fun

2 monkeys ate 3 bananas each. 4 monkeys ate 2 bananas each.

How many bananas did the monkeys eat in all?

Name:

Work Space:

Answer:

_____ bananas

Name:

Monkey Fun

Carmen wants to buy a book about monkeys.
She has this much money:

Circle the book that Carmen can buy with the money she has.

| $4.55 | $4.95 | $5.10 |

Daily Word Problems

Monday-Week 29

Vacation

We are going camping in three weeks.

How many days is that?

Name:

Work Space:

Answer:

_____ days

Daily Word Problems

Tuesday-Week 29

Vacation

Gas for the car costs $26. Food costs $40. The campsite costs $25.

How much will the trip cost?

Name:

Work Space:

Answer:

$_____

Daily Word Problems

Wednesday-Week 29

Vacation

We drove for 2 hours, stopped half an hour for lunch, and swam at the lake for half an hour.

How long did it take to get to the campsite?

Name:

Work Space:

Answer:

_____ hours

Daily Word Problems

Thursday-Week 29

Vacation

It took my dad 30 minutes to set up our tents.

If he started at 4:15, at what time did he finish?

Name:

Work Space:

Show your answer on the clock.

Answer:

_____ : _____

Name:

Vacation

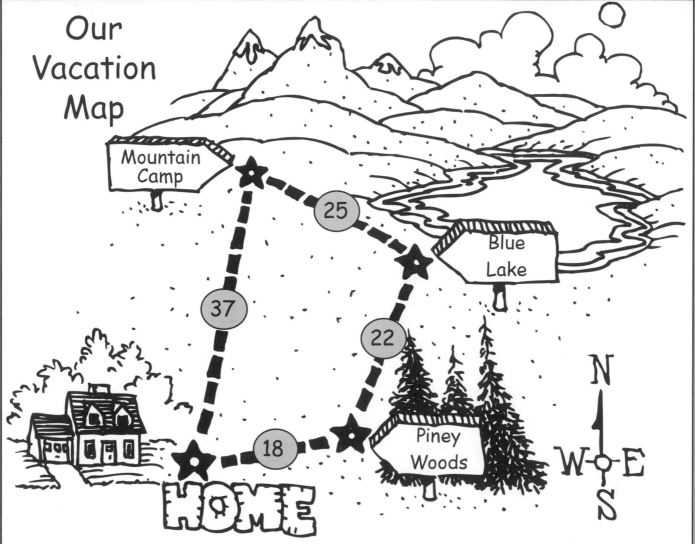

Our Vacation Map

Mountain Camp

25

Blue Lake

37

22

18

Piney Woods

HOME

N
W   E
S

1. Today we drove from home to Piney Woods and stopped for lunch. Then we drove to Blue Lake. We stopped to swim for a while. Then we drove to Mountain Camp.

   How many miles did we drive today? _____ miles

2. On Sunday we drove home from Mountain Camp the quickest way. How many miles did we drive? _____ miles

3. How many fewer miles did we travel going home than going to Mountain Camp? _____ miles

Daily Word Problems

Monday–Week 30

Row the Boat

12 parents, 16 girls, and 22 boys rode to the lake on a bus.

How many people were going to the lake?

Name:

Work Space:

Answer:

_____ people

Daily Word Problems

Tuesday–Week 30

Row the Boat

The bus left at 8:05. The trip took 20 minutes.

At what time did the bus arrive at the lake?

Name:

Work Space:

Show your answer on the clock.

Answer:

_____ : _____

Daily Word Problems

Row the Boat

Each boat had one pair of oars.

How many oars were there for these boats?

Name:

Work Space:

Answer:

4 boats = _____ oars

8 boats = _____ oars

3 boats = _____ oars

6 boats = _____ oars

Daily Word Problems

Row the Boat

It cost $5.00 an hour to rent a boat.

1. How much would it cost to rent a boat for 2 hours?

2. How much would it cost to rent a boat for 4 hours?

Name:

Work Space:

Answer:

1. $_____ for 2 hours

2. $_____ for 4 hours

There were rowboat races on the lake all day.
The names of the winning boats were shown on a sign.
The winner of each race won $10.00 and a ribbon.
The winner of the most races won $100.00 more and a trophy.

The Winners!

The blue boat won 3 races.

The yellow boat won 4 races.

The red boat won 5 races.

The green boat won 1 race.

The silver boat won 4 races.

1. How many races took place? _____ races

2. Which boat won the most races? _____ boat

3. How much money did the crew of
   that boat win? $_____

Daily Word Problems

Monday-Week 31

Crawly Critters

Stan, Fran, and Dan went on an insect hunt in the backyard. They saw 26 ladybugs, 9 butterflies, 2 grasshoppers, and 23 ants.

How many insects did they see in all?

Name:

Work Space:

Answer:

_____ insects

Daily Word Problems

Tuesday-Week 31

Crawly Critters

A line of ants was crawling on and around Stan's sandwich. "I'll bet there are 325 ants on my sandwich," said Stan. "And there must be 550 ants coming in a line."

How many ants did Stan guess there were in all?

Name:

Work Space:

Answer:

_____ ants

Daily Word Problems

Wednesday-Week 31

Crawly Critters

Stan, Dan, and Fran saw a spider catch a fly in its web.

If the spider ate 4 flies every day, how many flies would it eat in a week?

Name:

Work Space:

Answer:

_____ flies

Daily Word Problems

Thursday-Week 31

Crawly Critters

Pretend that a spider and a fly were wearing shoes.

1. How many shoes would they need in all?

2. How many pairs of shoes would they need?

Name:

Work Space:

Answer:

1. _____ shoes

2. _____ pairs of shoes

One night Dan, Fran, and Stan caught fireflies in jars.
Dan caught 12. Fran caught twice as many as Dan.
Stan caught half as many as Dan.

1. How many fireflies did Fran catch? _____ fireflies

2. How many fireflies did Stan catch? _____ fireflies

3. How many more did Fran catch than Stan? _____ fireflies

4. How many fireflies did they catch in all? _____ fireflies

Daily Word Problems

Monday–Week 32

A New Home

Kim and her dad built a new home for their dog, Buddy. It took Kim and Dad 24 minutes to build the floor and 68 minutes to build the walls.

How long did they work?

Name:

Work Space:

Answer:

_____ minutes

Daily Word Problems

Tuesday–Week 32

A New Home

Kim and Dad used small pieces of wood to make a roof for Buddy's doghouse. There were 30 pieces of wood. Dad and Kim used 14 pieces.

How many pieces of wood were left?

Name:

Work Space:

Answer:

_____ pieces of wood

Daily Word Problems • EMC 300

Daily Word Problems

Wednesday-Week 32

A New Home

Kim and Dad bought two cans of paint for the doghouse. The green paint cost $4.35 and the white paint cost $3.52.

How much did the paint cost in all?

Name:

Work Space:

Answer:

$_____

Daily Word Problems

Thursday-Week 32

A New Home

Kim bought a new water dish that said "Buddy." The new water dish cost $3.75. Kim gave the clerk $4.00.

How much money did Kim have left?

Name:

Work Space:

Answer:

$_____

Daily Word Problems

Friday-Week 32

Name: _____

A New Home

Buddy gets dog cookies every day.

This graph shows how many cookies Buddy ate last week.

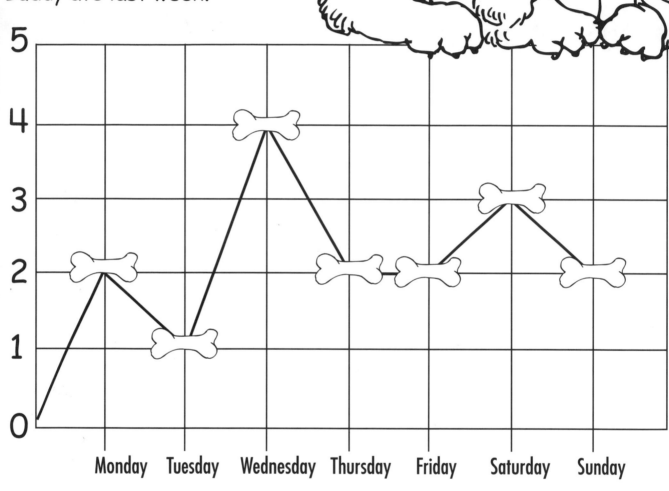

1. How many dog cookies did Buddy eat last week?

   _____ dog cookies

2. Kim opened a new box of dog cookies last Monday. A box holds 30 cookies. How many cookies were left at the end of the week?

   _____ dog cookies

Daily Word Problems • EMC 300: